Relax Into Inspired

Action:

Connect the Pieces,

and Live Fulfilled

By

Dr. Sheri Kaye Hoff, PhD.

Your Path to Success Enterprises, LLC

www.lifeisjoyful.org

Copyright 2015

DEDICATION

This book is dedicated to everyone who is connecting the pieces in their lives that lead to fulfilling purpose and making a difference in the world. To every person who has ever felt unworthy. To every person who dared to dream in spite of fear. To every person who has felt fear and decided to face it and overcome it. To every person who keeps taking steps forward, learning and growing. I appreciate you and honor your journey.

Thank you to Joanna, Bonnie, Maryann, and Vivienne for your contributions to Relax into Inspired Action: Connect the Pieces and Live Fulfilled. Thank you to everyone in my coaching community.

In Happiness,

Sheri

TABLE OF CONTENTS

Foreword   7

Chapter 1: Introduction   9

Chapter 2: Connect the Pieces, Live   13

Fulfilled

Chapter 3: Master Your Inner game: 39

Freedom, Happiness, and Inspired Action

Chapter 4: Achieving Goals and Living   87

Your Success

Chapter 5: Relax Into Attracting Clients   123

and Relax Into Profits

Chapter 6: Conclusion   131

About the Author   133

FOREWORD

By Actress and Award Winning Producer

Joanna Sanchez

I am so grateful for all that I have learned working with the most amazing and brilliant Dr. Sheri Kaye Hoff. **She is a wonderful support and guide for me.** I am an actress and producer with a career in the arts. I have a big vision for my life.

Sheri has taught me to hold onto the vision while keeping in the most positive vibration, becoming crystal clear knowing all that I want to attract. I repeat often the mantra she has taught me "Everything is always

working out for me"...This sustains me as I go through my day.

We create inspired action steps while removing any limiting or negative thought patterns. Sheri has helped me see certain distractions that have held me back for so long. **Sheri has taught me to be in my brilliance each day,** eliminating doubts and fears. I have never felt more ready to step into my stardom in all areas of my life. I am in deep gratitude for this beautiful angel in my life, Dr Sheri Kaye Hoff.

Much love,

Joanna

Chapter 1

INTRODUCTION

The harder you work, the better your results.

It takes hard work to be successful.

*If you want to be successful, it's going to be really hard
and you will have to give up what you really would
rather be doing.*

Do any of the above thoughts seem familiar?

You, like many people, probably feel at times like you
are trapped into a never ending cycle of working harder
and harder; and sometimes it feels like there are even
less results. We think the equation should be:

*Work really hard to create a great life and make
more money.*

Often the equation is:

*Work really hard for a little bit of money, and
no time to do what you want to do.*

Now, don't get me wrong; I am actually a fan of effort. I grew up in a family with a strong work ethic. However, I have found that **there is a difference in the type of action you take and the results that you receive**.

My definition of action that gets the results you desire – is **relaxed inspired action-** not desperate action or desperate reaction.

Over my years as a coach and my experience in training and development, I have witnessed and cultivated a process called **connecting the pieces and living fulfilled**.

During this process you learn to put together all of the pieces that make you feel alive and passionate in your life into a business or career where you make a meaningful difference and are well compensated for your contribution to this world.

In this book, I highlight three *connecting the pieces stories* from remarkable women who have crafted their successful, fulfilling lives from the pain, suffering, and experiences that could have left them floundering. You will be inspired by them.

In addition, I share the **core beliefs, action steps, and wisdom** that will help you create your own connecting the pieces story.

If you are already in the process of connecting the pieces, you will fine tune and find ways to thrive and monetize what you are doing.

You will be motivated to take **massive relaxed inspired action steps.** (Just because it is relaxed, doesn't mean it can't be massive).

You will be able to use these techniques to **attract clients, grow your business, get happier, make a meaningful contribution, and become more successful.**

You will learn the main things that are blocking you from your success, and you will learn how to be **masterful with your inner-game** (your mindset, your emotions, and your spirit).

Are you ready to Relax into Inspired Action?

And are you ready to Connect the Pieces and Live Fulfilled?

Chapter 2

CONNECT THE PIECES AND LIVE

FULFILLED

Living a Heart-Centered Life and Thriving

Questions that I have been most interested in studying over the years are:

- What truly inspires regular, ordinary people to live extraordinary lives?

- How do people put together their lives in a way that fills them up with a sense of purpose and meaning?

- What drives people to thrive during challenging situations?

- How do people live heart centered lives without sacrificing their financial well-being?

I am awed by my experiences seeing people close up, raw, and deeply connected to their commitments to find a way to put together their lives so that they do what they love and succeed.

Creativity and a willingness to look at choices with a completely different perspective appear to be two of the keys to this process of living fulfilled.

Examples:

- A woman, who wants to be an author, starts their own publishing company and not only publishes his or her own book, but helps others to do the same and live their dreams.
- An individual who sees a desperate need and starts an event planning company to help non-profit organizations to raise funds.

- A person who sees an educational need for young women and creates a website that provides this vital information and training.

- The person who realizes after a near death experience that there is so much left to do and be.

As you seek to live with meaning and purpose, ask yourself these questions:

- What do I love?

- What feels natural?

- What do I do that I wish I could make money or more money doing?

- What makes me feel most alive?

- What makes me feel like I am using my gifts?

- When am I most fulfilled?

The above questions will help you discover more about your passion and purpose.

The questions below will help you realize what is holding you back:

- What makes me feel tired as soon as I think of it?

- Where do I feel I make most of my mistakes?

- What feels exhausting?

- What do I wish would go away?

Start releasing, letting go, deleting or delegating items from the second list.

Journal Prompt:

How important is it for me to live a fulfilling life? What do I feel and think it will take to get me there?

If you are not using a journal, how about starting one? Many of my clients have found that it is a valuable tool for change and growth. Writing even one sentence a day helps.

Create synergy and momentum in your life by looking at these areas of your life:

- Your theme for your year. This is one word or phrase that serves as a slogan for what you are trying to accomplish. Some past themes I have used for myself have been "Alignment", "Abundance". "Be the Inspiration" "Be Bold" "Relaxed Success".

- Your goals. Review the goals that you have set making sure they are goals that really light up your life and make you want to jump out of bed every day.

- Your daily practice. Momentum grows exponentially as you practice new habits and inspired action every day.

- Your people. Be around energetic, positive, life affirming people.

- Your team. Create a team with trust, unity, and vision.

Synergistic practices:

- **The Universe Likes Speed- Allow that things can happen fast.**

- Daily Journal. Write in your journal every day.

- Daily Gratitude. Feel appreciation every day by saying thank you.

- Daily Love. Allow love in and give love. Use loving language.

- Daily Learning. Learn something new as part of your daily practice.

- Daily Movement and Nourishment. Any movement is positive and choose foods that make you feel energized and renewed.

- Daily accountability. Track and share your progress with your coach, a friend, or a mentor.

- The importance of 'I am" "I am" is the creative force. Use the feeling and meaning of these words wisely and unleash your powerful potential

- Be the energy of what you want. Increase your energy vibration. Stay focused on high energy thoughts and actions.

My own Connecting the Pieces story:

My clients know me as "action Sheri". I have owned my company since 2007, my books are available internationally, my podcast is global, and I work with my ideal clients every day. I take vacations (lots of vacations). I feel spiritually connected and happy. I golf. I read books. I hang out with friends. I am close to my husband and children and involved in their lives...

But it wasn't always this way. I didn't always have it together. (And I don't always have it together every minute of the day, now).

What drove me to carve out the life I live today? Pain.

My own world was shattered when I was 17 and I came home from school one day to find my younger brother after his suicide death. **My identity was lost. I lost trust in everything (even God). It felt like I was on shaky ground all of the time.** Our family was grief stricken. However, I did have one glimmer of light... I knew at a deep level... that I would not let this beat me. I would get up again. I would survive. I didn't imagine ever being truly happy. I thought, if I got to OK, where I didn't cry every day, I would be doing pretty good. I still went to college. I still went to work. I had some fantastic people in my life that lifted me up when I stumbled.

Then one day, I didn't need to be lifted up anymore. I was on the road to getting better. I was okay.

My world shifted again when I was pregnant with my first daughter in 1994. I was on bed-rest and my mother gave me a copy of Steven Covey's 7 Habits book. And it was the first time since my brother died, that I made the connection regarding the power of thoughts. This book set me on a path of self-discovery and personal growth. I was inspired to continue my schooling earning my Master's and my PhD. **I made it**

my life-long quest to discover what makes people happy and why some people are successful and other's struggle.

I made the connection between thoughts and happiness. It was like a light bulb turned on and I realized that I could be happy if I decided to be happy. I even wrote my first book on happiness, **Keys to Living Joyfully**. I not only was okay, I was happy.

My early career was a hodge-podge of jobs with each one teaching me something about myself. Eventually, I moved to a career in management, and then I made the move to a career in higher education, and then training and development.

I felt, still, like I was missing something. I prayed and meditated about it. I woke up one morning in 2007 and knew I would start my own coaching and training company. I have never looked back. I had a learning curve and many challenges. It took me months to land my first client. **I cried tears of frustration in the beginning.** I had to learn how to market my own business which was much more challenging than sales and marketing for someone else. I had to work on my own sense of worthiness and conquer my fears, but it was exciting. It was exactly what I wanted to be doing. **I thrived as I saw my clients change their lives and grow their businesses.**

After a couple years of growing my company, I had another realization. **I was working too many hours**. There was a part of me that felt that I had to work really hard for success. I just couldn't do it anymore, though.

I needed more balance. I dug deep, and I decided that **I was going to do all of the things I really wanted to do.** If that meant golfing three times a week or taking frequent vacations, I was going to do it.

My business didn't miss a beat. In fact, it grew. When I was taking care of me and having fun, the energy of my business responded to that. I am still a queen of action, but I am relaxed about it. And I only act when I am in the inspired action state.

Every choice has a purpose. Every move is deliberate. I am deliberating creating my business and life every day.

Dr. Sheri Kaye Hoff, PhD.

Business Coach and Author

www.lifeisjoyful.org

Please enjoy three more stories from remarkable women in business.

Connecting the Pieces story by Maryann Candito

As I reflect back on my childhood, I was always the chubby little Italian girl with big hopes and dreams. Being an emotional Pisces as well as being highly sensitive, it was challenging to put my dreams into perspective and not get caught up in discouraging but "sensible and realistic" words of the adults I looked up to. **So I convinced myself that they were simply that – unattainable dreams. However a part of me still believed.**

I believed in the magic of the universe. I believed in miracles. I believed in something more. But for the longest time I couldn't connect the pieces.

Being such a sensitive person, I used food to deal with the heavy emotions that I felt. Being Italian, I used food for celebration, consolation, a symbol of love and family, recreation, comfort, and fun. You name it, Italian is synonymous with food. Food became my pleasure as much as it became my pain. At 13 years old I weighed 195 pounds. I went on my first diet. I lost some weight, but that was the start of the vicious yo-yo dieting that would be my life. Over the next 37 years I would lose 30-40 pounds over and over, only to gain much of it back. By the time I was 49 years old, facing mood swings, chocolate cravings, and hot flashes, I found myself, once again 35 pounds overweight.

Something changed for me this time. I refused to go on another diet. **I was determined to figure out the key to natural weight release without dieting**. In less than a year I released 35 pounds naturally, and have kept it off. I discovered that diets fail because they only focus on the physical – the body – the food. But we are so much more than that and that's how I broke the code! Now it's my mission to help others succeed as well. I am passionately committed to helping others transform their bodies, their minds, and their lives, without resorting to diets or deprivation. **My dreams are coming to fruition.** I'm a published author. I am a coach and speaker, and through this work, I am able to help people all over the world see their dreams of being healthy and empowered, come true.

If I hadn't experienced years of food struggles and weight issues, I never would've discovered my purpose in this world. I am living my dream of being of service while at the same time of having the freedom that I need so very much in my life. It's life on my terms. Fortunately I never lost touch with that little spark of the magical! **I BELIEVED, even though it was buried deep at times.** With each set-back over the years, I would lose hope and become discouraged. Often times I would ignore it, and go back to an unfulfilling job, convincing myself that this was simply life. But that wasn't good enough for me. I wanted more. And every now and again I would be reminded that I could have more, I could *be* more. I didn't have to let failures and set-backs define me and hold me back from what I was meant to do in this world. So I persevered. I trusted. **And I reawakened the magic!** Maryann Candito is a coach, speaker, and author of the book *I'm Losing It! 7 Steps to Jump Off the Diet Rollercoaster, Release Weight & Be in Charge Over Food.* www.synergyweightrelease.com

Connecting the Pieces story by Vivienne Smith

Once upon a time I was perfectly happy - complacent, even. I had a beloved husband and two sons, aged three years old and three weeks old. **But then my world came crashing down** and I was suddenly a single mum, losing sleep over how to pay the bills. My health suffered and my weight yoyo-ed as I tried to get my life in order. Worse was to come and I plucked up the courage to escape a disastrous second marriage to a sometimes charming, yet abusive man.

Even in the depths of the darkest days of my life, I felt a growing conviction that I was going to survive this and reach back and help other women in similar situations to thrive despite – or even *because of*- what had happened. Luckily, I'd done a lot of personal development through books and CDs and with the help of skilled practitioners. The things I learned allowed me to retain my sanity, self-esteem and sense of humour and to help my children get through the experience. I discovered how to release the emotions that were holding me back, get my weight under control and **find more fun, fulfilment and balance in my life (not to mention my lovely third husband!)**

I have always been curious and creative, a quick learner. This can be a disadvantage because I've kept my choices open and resisted being put into any particular box. Having worked as an image consultant, beauty salon manageress, presenter, artist and teacher I finally realised that I wanted to combine my existing skills and life experience and qualify in NLP (Neuro Linguistic Programming) and Hypnotherapy. **After years of searching for career fulfilment, for me it's the perfect fit** of teaching, creativity and empowering women to overcome their challenges and achieve their goals. I also found it to be the perfect way of turning my own personal trials, trauma and triumphs- into a gift I could share with others.

Way back in 2000 I had toyed with the idea of transforming my life as a single mother and some of my (often hilarious) internet dating experiences into a tragi-comic novel – a kind of Bridget Jones goes Internet Dating, if you will. But time pressures and real life got in the way and I worried that my two precious sons might be embarrassed by the whole idea anyway, so I shelved my manuscript. **I started doing a lot of**

business networking to launch my coaching business and continued studying.

Two modules in to an online marketing course, I discovered that writing a book on your specialist subject is a great way to position yourself as an expert in your field.

I had a brainwave: it was time to repurpose my book and fill it with a mixture of down-to-earth advice on every aspect of becoming and being a single mum: real life stories, encouragement and inspiration (the kind of book I'd so desperately needed all those years ago, but hadn't found on the bookshelves). I found that I had a compelling story to tell – and I also found it easy to connect with other women and encourage them to tell me their stories.

Through my business networking I met every single expert I needed, from legal and financial professionals to parenting and fitness experts. In 2014 I published my book, THE SINGLE MUM'S

SURVIVAL GUIDE- How To Pick Up The Pieces and

Build a Happy New Life. These days I divide my time

between coaching and presenting; I am also a Regional

Director for The Athena Network, a business women's

networking group.

Vivienne Smith

www.thesinglemumssurvivalguide.com

Connecting the Pieces story by Bonnie Gortler

I am honored to be part of "Relax into Inspired

Action: Connect the Pieces, Live Fulfilled" sharing my

story with all of you. Sheri is a leader, a true

inspiration who inspires you to be bold, brave, and

daring to achieve what you never imagined possible.

Sheri's love that she shares from her heart inspires you

to take action, feel more peace, passion, success and joy in life.

I have been a successful stock market expert for over 30 years. **Financial fitness is what I know best, but I have learned without your health there is no wealth.**

The challenge of the stock market has kept me thriving and alive on the outside, but **I was in pain on the inside.** I felt sad, angry, and numb after losing family, friends, to cancer including my mom at the age of 62. I spent years holding my feelings inside, as I drowned myself in my work.

Another tragedy occurred and in an instant my life changed unexpectedly. My mother-in-law, who I love dearly, became paralyzed. All of the muscles in her body collapsed. She was only able to move her hands from side to side, speak, and nothing more. An important message was given: life is short, live life to

www.lifeisjoyful.org

the fullest. Most doctors gave up on her, but she continued to fight for survival, recovery, and is enjoying life.

Then, a new world opened for me, my life as an entrepreneur began. Instant success turned into immediate failure, which became the ultimate breakthrough for me. I was asked a question "Why are you so negative?" In that moment, **I knew that the fearful, non-confident, stressed woman I was, needed to change**, but I had no idea how. Negativity and stress had to go. Change was necessary!

It was time to leave my comfort zone. I chose to hire my first coach. I began first by changing my words, my attitude, and raising my level of awareness. I never gave up on myself, no matter how much pain I felt. My coach suggested opening a Twitter account which opened my eyes to social media and life changed.

I found a trainer over the internet who educated me about the importance of self-care and my health and well-being journey began. I became interested in healthy eating and passionate for fitness. I found more coaches that inspired, supported, and challenged me to grow.

I took baby steps to reach my new goals. I added journaling to my hobbies, which helped to let go of the past and the beliefs that were limiting me. **I changed my vocabulary from "I can't," "I won't," and "I fear,"... to "I can!"** I realized that my new-found spirit would overtake my fears.

Fire and desire from my heart took over. **I learned everything is a choice.** When I first started writing I could barely write a business letter or a blog. Sheri inspired, supported, and encouraged me to press on. I began reading more books, taking courses, engaging in group programs, and mastermind groups.

Being open, willing to step out of my comfort zone and asking for guidance is a key step to growth to do what you never imagined you could or would do. I was persistent until completion and published my book "Journey to Wealth" and my life coaching certification.

A positive attitude, a winning mindset and to dream big is possible. The journey continues, sharing my insights, to create change in lives of many, all around the world who struggle with building wealth, and having compassion about their well-being so they can enjoy life again.

Investing in your own personal development sometimes can be a bit scary. Never give up on what you are passionate about doing. The risk is worth the reward.

Invest in YOU! Live the healthy, wealthy lifestyle that you desire.

Bonnie Gortler

Wealth and Well-Being Coach

www.bonniegortler.com

As you read these stories of these amazing women, you can see a few common traits and the most glaring similarity is all of these women mastered their inner-game. They were able to still the inner voice of criticism and overcome obstacles, and discover fulfillment, happiness, and success.

Chapter 3

MASTER YOUR INNERGAME:

FREEDOM, HAPPINESS, AND INSPIRED

ACTION

Your inner-game is a determinant for your ultimate results and your success in your life. Consider these questions:

- **What beliefs run your life and are they working for you or against you?**

- Are your emotions and mental attitudes attracting results at a high or low energetic level?

- Are you confident in your decision-making and your ability to get the results you want?

If you want to be able to take more inspired action, experience higher level results, feel more confident and let go of fear getting in the way of what you really want to do; master your inner game.

Why do some people succeed? And others, even though they seem to have the skills, talents and potential, never really get going and experience the success they really want? I have been studying this topic for over 20 years and the key to results is your inner game. Your inner game determines much of your success. What makes up your inner game? Mindset. Beliefs. Emotional Intelligence. Spirituality. Your inner game is what carries you through your challenges or lets you get stuck in your challenges.

Right now, is the crucial time to commit to keep moving forward on your goals. Master your inner game. You have some terrific goals and you probably began your approach **with lots of enthusiasm**, by now you have made progress, but the truth is you may also have experienced a few dips or setbacks, too. This is completely normal, but don't be discouraged or start worrying whether this will be your year or not to really breakthrough to the level of happiness and success you desire.

You can. You can get the results you want.

Pause here and ask yourself, "What would my life look life if I started getting the results I want in my biz or life? What difference would it make to me?"

I am sharing inner game lessons and exercises in this section that have helped me and my clients get the results they want.

Are you worried about whether or not you really can achieve your results, and are you basing this on the fact that you may have a few "fails" in the past?

No one likes the word "failure" and no one wants to ever experience failure... but the truth is that our failures pave the way for our eventual success and we have only truly failed if we stop trying. I actually change the wording in my own life and for my clients... I use the word "lessons" instead of "failures".

Some of my biggest "failures" (lessons) have led to my best experiences in my life. My clients are able to see this in their lives, too. They stop beating themselves up because something didn't work, and then they ask, "How can I tweak this?" "What changes do I need to make?"

When you truly decide and commit, you can make anything happen. You can get from where you are now to where you want to be. What will it take for you to make the changes that you want?

It doesn't matter where you come from, what your past has been, or any other external factor... the difference maker begins with a thought, then a decision.

Change Your Story

When you change your story that you tell about yourself, you change your life. You can start telling a better story right now.

The Three Biggest Blocks to Your Success: Time, Money, Fear

If you want to know what is in your way look at these three topics: time, money, and fear. You can change your story about these three topics.

Your approach to time affects your success and inner peace on a daily basis, your thoughts and beliefs about money impact your financial situation every day, and fear is what keeps you from taking the actions steps that you really want to take. **What if** you felt like you had all of the time you want to do what you want? What if you didn't worry about money? What if fear didn't keep you from making the changes that you want?

Recently at one of my 2 day virtual retreats with some of my business coaching clients, we tackled these big three topics on day 1. Everyone craved to get the time, money, fear thing handled. What happened? **People shifted**. They moved into a better feeling and being place around these topics.

Let's look at time first. Honestly, the biggest excuse is "I don't have enough time". I even chuckle a little bit on the inside when I hear it, or I hear myself saying it. I used to be over-scheduled, constantly looking at my watch, and packing so much into my day that the only way to find more time was to keep shaving off my sleeping time. I was tired and burned out. I viewed time from a place of lack. I often wished for more time in a day; though secretly I knew this wouldn't help me out because I would just add even more activity.

Then, I had a **mindset shift** about the concept of time several years ago. I thought what if I viewed time the same way as I was beginning to view the Universe- as abundant. What if I viewed my schedule from a place of deliberate creator or CEO of my own life, instead of feeling like a victim of my schedule? I asked myself, What if I could do the things I really wanted to be doing? I began to view time in a completely different way.

Did you know that time, as we know it, was created by man? If you doubt this, take a look at daylight savings time. A few people got together and decided- "let's move time forward and back twice a year". Also, who decided exactly where each time zone changes? And who decided that there were 24 hours in a day? Someone- a person- decided. Quantum physics tells us that time doesn't exist the way we think it does. So why let it rule our lives? Instead, be a master of your life. Look at what is most important to you, and do that. For every one thing you want to add, take away 2 things (delegate or eliminate).

"Either you run the day, or the day runs you" – Jim Rohn

I like time for spontaneous creativity, so I schedule big blocks on my calendar that are empty. When I get to the empty spots, I let them be whatever I want them to be in the moment. The greatest thing that gives me peace about time is knowing that I get to make choices about what I do with it. I also find it amazing that when there is something I really want to do, I find the time for it. If you shifted your beliefs and choices about time, how would that change your day?

What about money? How can you handle that money struggle in your life? The answer lies in how you feel about money and how you feel about the likelihood of abundance coming your way.

The key is to shift your mindset and feelings away from "struggle", and towards feeling better and better about your money and finances. Feeling good is a vibe that brings your goals and desires to you. But what do you when you are feeling bad? Pay attention to the feeling, notice the feeling, examine the feeling, and accept the feeling. As you accept all of your feelings, you allow yourself to process them instead of stuff them down only to have them bubble up later. As you process your feeling, you will notice the belief that is driving the feeling.

Underneath a feeling, is a core thought and belief.

When you find yourself in struggle, ask- what is the belief here? For example your belief might be, I'm not good enough or I am terrible at managing my money, etc. Once you see what the belief is, you can shift it energetically through meditation, prayer, tapping, energy healing, journaling, affirmations, etc. Decide what the replacement belief will be for you. This is important.

As you release a belief that doesn't serve you, you want to lock in a new belief that is powerful.

A powerful new belief might be: I am a great money manager, I am worthy, etc. You can lock it in through writing affirmations, EFT, visualization, meditation, or prayer or other energetic exercises. This is an energetic process. It is important to truly shift the belief instead of trying to talk yourself out of a belief. In my coaching groups, we work with many techniques that create immediate shifts. Members of my tribe often experience changes in the moment. It doesn't need to take weeks, months, or years to have profound shifts.

You don't need to go over every detail of your past, but if something comes up, face it and process those feelings, get to the core belief, so you can shift it.

"Look for good things about where you are, and in your state of appreciation, you lift all self-imposed limitations - and all limitations are self-imposed - and you free yourself for the receiving of wonderful things." Abraham Hicks

Money flows in when you are not thinking about having to get money. Money flows in from multiple sources, when you are truly focused on feeling good about what you are doing and living the present moment fully. If you think it has to be hard, then it is hard; if you decide it can be easy, natural, and flowing-you have opened the door.

Finally, let's turn our attention to fear, the last of the big three we are discussing here today. What prevents you from taking the action steps you know you want to take? Most likely, the answer is fear. You probably have many reasons (excuses) for not taking the action steps, but underneath all of those reasons are fear. You could be feeling fear of failure, fear of success, fear of rejection, fear of judgment, or fear of _____ (fill in the blank).

In order to understand how fear operates in your life, reflect back over the choices you have made.

Notice how fear impacted your choices. Did you choose to apply to an easier college because you were afraid you might not get accepted? Did you take a job with less pay and less demands because you were afraid to go for what you really wanted? Did you wait to start your business, because you were afraid you might not make it in business? Did you pass up a networking opportunity because you were afraid? Did you downshift out of success, because suddenly you feared what big success might mean in your life?

What if you didn't have any of that fear? Or when that fear came up, you just handled it?

What impact will it have on your business and your life, if you could successfully overcome any fear that operates in your life?

What is fear anyway? It doesn't exist. It is not a thing. It is only a thought/feeling that you create in your mind. Past experiences ingrain fear sometimes. **If you experienced rejection as a child (and who didn't?), some of your fear is tied to that.**

I made a decision in my own life, to face everything that made me feel uncomfortable or fearful.

I decided that I didn't want fear driving my decisions any longer.

I also noticed that I felt fear right before a big breakthrough. This made me almost look forward to the fear experience, because I knew it meant I was doing something great. I also shifted my thoughts to seeing fear as an adventure. We feel fear when we go on a roller coaster, but it ends up being fun.

How can you process fear, when it seems paralyzing? In your present moment of fear, notice if it resembles any other fear experiences that you had in your life. Go to a prior experience, and let yourself be fully in the moment. If you were a child, and were bullied, you probably shut down and didn't feel your feelings. As you are in the moment of your past fear, see if you can feel it in your body somewhere. We carry our repressed feelings in the body. It might be your stomach, your liver, your throat, etc. Also notice if it has a color. Take some deep breaths, and allow it to expand to as big as it wants to get. Keep deep breathing. As you focus your attention on the body, see the feeling or imagine the feeling breaking up in front of your eyes and dissolving. Practice this exercise anytime powerful fear comes up for you. Then take your action step. You've released fear, so you are free to move forward and do the thing you feared.

Another self-awareness tip is to be able to connect discomfort in your life or indecision to an operating fear. What is the underlying fear? Decide that you will face it. You are an adult, you are strong, and facing a fear and dissolving it- is liberating.

Another approach for dealing with fear is to make a decision to take action despite the fear. The only way to conquer a fear of riding a bike is to do it. You probably have heard the expression, feel the fear and do it anyway. Taking action builds confidence and reduces fear.

"Thinking will not overcome fear but action will." ~W. Clement Stone

Effectively changing your time, money, and fear stories frees **you to create your magic, to be the highest version of yourself.**

Beating Overwhelm and Managing Your Emotions: Change your Overwhelm Story.

Overwhelm hits us when we have a lot going on and/or are in the midst of change. Did you know that the state of overwhelm can become a habitual story you tell about yourself? And you can change this story and change your life, too.

The problem with feeling overwhelmed is that the mind spins and this can have a paralyzing and severely demoralizing effect.

It feels toxic to spend time in this emotional place. You might even feel trapped.

Here are **some tips for handling overwhelm** so you can do more of what you really want to be doing on a daily basis.

1. **Let go**. Stop trying to control the world. We begin a project with an idea of what will happen, and

when we get surprised; there is that inclination to feel frustrated. "Hey, this isn't fair. This isn't what I planned." Sound familiar? Let go of needing to control the situation. Try it- feel the release as you let go.

2. **Accept what is.** Whatever is going on- accept it rather than try to fight it. When you accept what is- then you are free to act. You have the energy to take action. You haven't used up all of your energy trying to fight and force things into place. What we resist persists. You will know you are in resistance when you look at what you are trying hard to push away and out of your life. Or when you are busy doing everything except for what you really know you want to be doing. **What are you resisting today?** Many of us resist emotions. We do not like to feel anger, fear, frustration, sadness, etc. We do almost everything we can to avoid addressing and accepting these emotions. This only prolongs the emotions and does nothing to

soothe and shift your emotions. Today, instead of trying to fight off those emotions, allow yourself to fully feel and honor what is. When we accept what is... we have a starting point for change and greater inner peace.

Exercise:

State- here is where I am... (*state the emotion*). I fully honor this right now and allow myself to experience this moment.

Then, state:

I also honor that here is where I want to be.... (*state your desire*). Completing this exercise will help you be in a state of acceptance instead of resistance.

3. **Stop beating yourself up**. Release blame. It does not help you to go over and over what you think you should have done or said. Stop blaming other people too. You don't need to make yourself or other people "wrong" in order to deal with your life in the moment.

4. **Do what works.** This is so important. If you know that a long walk calms you down, do that. If you know that balancing your check book makes you feel more in control- do that. If you know that writing in your journal gives you clarity, do that.

5. **Do what you want to do and delegate the rest.** If you think you "should" be doing something but it feels forced or you don't like it- don't do it. For example, in my own situation regarding moving people in and moving people out- I realized that adults are empowered to plan their own moves. My daughters' planned and implemented everything (I was on hand to help- but I released my title- as Master of the Universe). On the other hand, if taking an action feels good and empowering, by all means, take action. Use this concept when dealing with long to-do lists.

6. **Release worry and guilt.** Worry and guilt are burdensome emotions. Love yourself and others

without worry and guilt attached. A simple exercise is to place your hand over your heart and concentrate on the feeling of love. Hold this position for a few minutes.

7. **Take care of your health**. Eat well, sleep well, move your body, take your vitamins, manage your stress, and pay attention to your needs.

Whenever you feel overwhelmed and are trying to decide what to do, ask yourself- "What is most important? What is my legacy?

The bottom line is to do what works for you and what you feel good about doing. Trust your inner guidance. Busy is good and healthy- overwhelm is not. Sometimes overwhelm can be a mask for resistance. As you practice healthy self-awareness, you will recognize resistance and take steps to manage it.

In addition to overwhelm, other emotions can wreak havoc on your daily plans. You set goals only to have your emotions interfere. Mastering emotions is an important key to success. Here are some additional methods to help you manage your emotions and live a life of intention rather than reaction. Even happy emotions can take you off your plan.

1. Recognition. Realize when emotions are taking you off-course.

2. Keep a journal of your actions throughout the day and notice how you are feeling.

3. Allow your feelings. If you notice that you are angry. Let yourself feel the anger instead of trying to numb yourself through a destructive coping mechanism.

4. Manage your stress. Decide ahead of time how you will manage your stress throughout the day. Will you take a walk? Get a massage? Listen to music? Hit golf balls? Take a nap?

5. Deal with the high pressure situations in your life. Create a strategy. If you have money problems,

seek a solution. If you have relationship problems face this. If you have health problems, do something about it.

6. Understand that you are always in a place where you have the power to choose rather than react.

Managing emotions is about living your truth rather than suffering a series of reactions.

You are a powerful creator and more than your emotions.

Emotions are a good guiding system to let you know what is going on inside; but they are not the rulers of your world. Appreciate your emotional range which is part of the wonderful human experience, but keep your inner guidance system in place.

Follow your path. Choose your destination.

Cultivate a Burning Desire

"When you discover your mission, you will feel its demand. It will fill you with enthusiasm and a burning desire to get to work on it." W. Clement Stone

What you need to almost guarantee success is burning desire. Authors W. Clement Stone assures us that without burning desire, you will not achieve a high level of success.

Burning desire is a rare thing.

Most people do not dare to cultivate a burning desire for anything because the second you allow a burning desire, there is a fears that get churned up. "What if I can't do it?" or "I don't know how to make it happen." or "What will people think?" are some fear related thoughts that may arise for you.

Why is it important to cultivate burning desire for your goal or goals? Burning desire is what carries you through when things go wrong or very, very slow. Burning desire keeps you going. Without burning desire you could end up stopping just when things are about to break open. Burning desire assures that you will cross the finish line.

If you have a goal and you feel like you have lost that burning desire or never really had it in the first place, **what do you need to do to get it?**

First, look at the real reason, the real why. This is why you want the goal. What difference will your dream make in your life and the lives of others?

Next, let yourself be filled with burning desire. Think about your goals as if they are really happening. See yourself achieving each phase of the goal. What does that feel like? Be the energy of your goal. It takes some practice, but as everyone who has ever achieved worthwhile goals realizes- it is worth the effort.

Let Your Suffering Become Your Strength

If you feel like you are suffering, your suffering can become your greatest strength. I recently had a fairly ordinary experience that ended up driving home the importance of transcending any condition and even turning it into a strength.

I was at the eye doctor with my daughter and we both needed new prescriptions. After spending nearly two hours there picking out new frames (my daughter is really particular about her appearance), we left. As we walked out to the car, Sonja observed that both the gentleman who helped us pick out the frames and the eye doctor had serious issues with their eyes. They both shared about having a severely dominant eye. My daughter concluded that they became eye doctors because they suffered with their vision. This is what made them **passionate** about their field.

I am sure that there are probably eye doctors with very little problems with their eyes, but this got me thinking. I remembered that my dermatologist shared that he struggled with acne for years and my dentist that I had when I was young- also had severe problems with his teeth when he was growing up.

I thought about my book, Keys to Living Joyfully which was part of my quest to find happiness after years of grief from the tragic loss of my brother. I thought about Viktor Frankl who inspired so many after he suffered in a concentration camp.

I was reminded to make the connection that **suffering inspires amazing work.** Not that one must suffer to be creative or make a contribution, but a person can take his or her deepest suffering and make it his or her mission and passion.

E.g. my own deep sadness prompted a quest for joy.

E.g. a person who struggles with food becomes an expert at weight loss.

E.g. a person who struggled being poor becomes an expert at making and managing money.

Light bulb moment: Look at any burden you are currently carrying as a potential mission for changing your life and the world.

If you wonder what your purpose is, what do you know best?

"Men are not prisoners of Fate, but only prisoners of their own minds.**" -Franklin Roosevelt**

Create Every Day Happiness

Happiness is not a someday thing; it is a now thing. Happiness is a practice. I view happiness as a lifestyle. You can choose happiness just like you can choose your clothes in your closet. Here are 5 tips that help me and my clients create every day happiness.

1. **Create a journaling practice.** (Notice I have mentioned journaling several times in this book already?) Journaling is for everyone, not just writers. Writing a few minutes a day will change your life. Here is the specific journaling method I used to create my own happiness. **Use an active approach which means that you are journaling for change and not just recording thoughts.** Write your gratitude list. Then write your manifestation/goals list. Then get quiet and listen to your inner voice for guidance and write down anything that comes up. Finish with a proclamation that you like such as, "All is well." "Thy will be done." "This or something better."

2. **Pay attention to your language**. Notice the words you speak throughout the day. Are you complaining or gossiping? This is a common habit and

habits can be changed. You may think you are positive, but how often do you refer to successful people as dishonest? Or confident people as arrogant? Or talented people as lucky? Or wealthy people as crooked? Or the world as messed up? And so on. Speak kind words as often as you can. When you must offer constructive criticism be matter of fact, calm, and logical.

3. **Be in the present moment.** The past is gone and the future uncertain. You have right now. Live in the moment. When you live in the past or future, you are missing the moment. Get present by noticing your feet on the ground and take deep breaths in and out. Observe your surroundings with great detail. **Practice being fully present several times a day.** You can set a timer, and then when the time goes off, spend 68 seconds on feeling good, happy and present.

4. **Touch and connect.** Hug people you love. Hold hands. Look into people's eyes when you are

talking to them. Connect with yourself and spirit through prayer and meditation.

5. **Help someone.** Donate time, give money, help a friend move, listen to a friend's troubles, or see a need and meet it. My daughter, at 16, saw a need when she went to LA for a week and worked with homeless people. When she returned home, she had a greater understanding of homelessness and started a project called Blankets for Denver where she and her friends collected blankets and donations for the Denver Rescue Mission.

To practice every day happiness pick something from this list and get started or choose your own method. Happiness is an everyday choice. How will you create your own every day happiness?

"Happiness is not a someday thing; it is a now thing." – Dr. Sheri Kaye Hoff, PhD

"Happiness is not something ready-made. It

comes from your own actions." – Dalai Lama

Live an inspired life.

What does being successful mean? We

witness some people with material success living

miserable lives. We witness spiritual people living lives

of poverty. Yet we also witness people with material

success living spiritually rich and physically healthy

lives.

Why do so many people live in the space of

tolerating their lives rather than living fully and

joyfully?

How can people transcend merely tolerating life

to living inspired lives?

According to Jack Canfield, "Scientists used to

believe that humans responded to information flowing

into the brain from the outside world. But today they're learning instead that we respond to what the brain, on the basis of previous experience, expects to happen next."

As a coach, I have talked with people who are miserable doing the work they do and they stay where they are month after month and year after year. I have talked with people who have even spent a million dollars on their education only to find that they made the wrong career choice based on what they should do instead of choosing something they love to do. I also have talked with people who have been downsized from their jobs and left to figure out what to do next, and to people who have filed bankruptcy. Often people come to me for coaching when they experience a stressor like a business crisis, a divorce, a health scare, a job loss, or a general feeling of wanting something better.

They want to live what I call an inspired life.

What does it mean to live an inspired life?

My own quest began because of a tragic experience that I had as a teenager. I was one of those people who tolerated life, and thought I would never be happy again. However, I learned that it truly is possible to live a joy filled, meaningful, and an inspired life. **Learning how to live inspired** has been part of a life-long quest of discovering success and happiness in my own life and then, in turn, allowing me to help my coaching clients do the same. I choose to live an inspired life, and I assist my coaching clients along the path to living inspired lives and **growing inspired businesses**.

Living an inspired life begins with knowing who you are and appreciating yourself.

Notice that the word wonderful is used in this scripture. "For you created in me my in most being: you knit me together in my mother's womb. I praise you because I am fearfully and wonderfully made: your works are wonderful, I know that full well." (NIV- New International Version, Psalms 139:13, 14).

You are made perfectly. You are a miracle.

Living an inspired life is possible through understanding the creative force of your mind. Your mind is powerful with unlimited potential for creation. With your thought, you put creation in motion (positive or negative). When you understand this power, you become a deliberate creator. You know that your life is the way it is because of what you have put into motion. Change your thoughts and you change your world.

Living an inspired life begins with knowing your relationship with God (Source, Universe). You were loved from the very beginning and are deeply loved now. "…We love because he first loved us." (NIV, 1 John 4:19).

You are already perfect love. You are one with God.

From the strength of being spiritually connected and being a master of your own thoughts, you are poised to take inspired action. I call this relaxed inspired action. This is **action that feels like a revelation instead of action** that is forced or reaction based.

"Living an inspired life begins with knowing who you are and appreciating yourself." – Dr. Sheri Kaye Hoff, PhD

"The only way to do great work is to love what you do. If you haven't found it yet, keep looking. Don't settle." – Steve Jobs

"All our dreams can come true – if we have the courage to pursue them." – Walt Disney

Releasing Worry

Do you worry? Constant worrying is an issue for many people. Worry keeps you up at night and keeps you from being and living in the present moment.

If you tend to worry, you even worry when things are going great. Most often you worry (in this situation) about what will happen when things stop going great.

The topics of your worries are non-issues since you tend to worry no matter what is going on.

I grew up with a Father who slept fitfully almost every night as worries from his highly stressful job and supporting the family pressed on him. I always thought my Dad worried because he had so much responsibility. Then I saw him in retirement and he continued worrying about his Sunday school class and his responsibilities at church and home. If a problem came up, he would agonize about every possible solution and he took on other people's burdens.

People say, you can't teach an old dog new tricks, but I have witnessed him improve and worry less over the past couple of years. We haven't really talked about it, but I suspect that as my Dad increased prayer in his life, his worry decreased.

Whether you pray or not, you can apply the principles of prayer which involve **relaxation, releasing, and allowing and you will find your worrying problem decrease.**

Relax your body. Release responsibility for the world. Let go. Allow God (Spirit, Higher Power, the Universe) to take over the burden. If you feel like you cannot change your worrying, remember that worrying is a form of prayer. Whatever you think about and dwell upon repeatedly is likely to materialize.

To stop your own worrying:

1.   **Interrupt your worry pattern** by noticing when you start worrying and then interrupt it with deep breaths, stretches, or even a distraction like a quick phone call, text, or a book.

2.   **When you are aware that you are worried, notice your muscles.** Are you clenching your hands? Is your forehead creased? Are you grinding your teeth? Are you tightening your pelvic floor? Are your feet tense? Mentally relax your muscles by imagining light flowing over your body and each muscle releases as the light flows over it.

3.   **Replace the worry thought** with a positive statement to help you move to a more empowering mindset. E.g. - If you are worried about money- use this statement, "Money comes to me, often, in many ways."

4.   Avoid checking email or opening mail right before you go to sleep.

5.   Set an intention before you fall asleep like- "When I wake up I will have a fresh perspective on this issue." And/or pray.

6.   Use ambient noise like a waterfall or ocean waves as you fall asleep.

7.   Recognize that you might need professional help if your worrying has turned into constant anxiety.

To stop others from worrying: (People are responsible for themselves, but you can provide a bit of relief with these steps).

1.   Don't find fault, blame or judge. (Especially children).

2.   Offer a distraction. For example, if your child is worried about a test- Try changing the subject by asking about their latest

basketball game, etc… (Whatever he or she is excited about in life). This really works well.

3.   Help the person see many alternative positive outcomes which helps avoid the situation of "all the eggs being in one basket".

4.   Let the person know that you care and are there to be supportive, but don't get tripped up in their worries.

5.   Suggest professional help if the worries seem persistent and abnormal.

Worrying is a thought habit and habits can be changed. When you change the worrying habit, you are able to enjoy life and deeply experience more peace, passion, energy, and joy. You are able shift away from worry and shift to the ability to **relax into inspired action**.

If You Release One Fear, You Can Release

Any Fear

My fear was ridiculous and I had been hiding behind it for years. You must be thinking that it was a huge, gigantic fear of something terrible. It was a fear of golfing. Okay, I can hear you giggling right now.

Learning to golf was on my bucket list. My husband golfs and my son golfs, so it seems like a no-brainer that I would golf, too. Or I would at least have plenty of opportunities to golf.

There is a story behind my ridiculous fear. Over 25 years ago, I was in a relationship and my boyfriend at the time took me to a golf tournament that he was golfing in. I told him I had never golfed and so the plan was that I would go and watch. When we arrived at the golf club, he decided that we would both hit balls at the driving range area.

The problem was… I couldn't hit the golf ball. I swung twice and missed it. My boyfriend looked so disgusted and he moved away from me. He pretended he didn't know me. I was 20 years old and embarrassed to be treated that way.

Fast forward a couple of decades, a husband, and kids… I began to crave to learn how to golf, but I really thought I couldn't do it. I have played many sports in my life- tennis, volleyball, downhill skiing, figure skating- just to name a few and have been naturally good at most sports.

I wanted to golf, but would get sweaty hands just thinking about it. I realized that I had let my early story really affect me. I wanted to break free from the story and finally put any hurt feelings from that previous relationship to rest.

I reasoned that eventually, I probably could hit a golf ball. I reasoned that even if I was terrible at golf, it would be okay. **Golfing became a symbol of doing everything in my life that I feared.** I decided to take the plunge and bought a set of clubs even before I had a lesson or even tried to hit a golf ball.

I went to the driving range with my husband and son. I swung at the first ball, and missed. Guess what? I didn't collapse into tears. The world didn't stop, and I still felt pretty darn good about myself. The second time I swung, I hit the ball; and it went about ten feet. Then I hit another, and another, and another. With each swing, I was getting better and better. I felt strong, powerful, and accomplished.

It turns out this was a start of a love affair with golf. I love it. I even watch it on TV, get Golf magazine, and have golf discussions with my husband and son. I am still a beginner. But I love being a beginner at something in my forties. Learning something new and being outside for hours has been wonderful for me.

Think about your life... and substitute the word golf for something you fear or have been putting off. Is there something you really want to do? Now is the time.

Choose Inner Peace

Inner peace is something that you can have in any given moment. **Having true inner peace begins with choosing it.** Make inner peace a daily choice. Commit to a life filled with inner peace. True inner peace means the outer circumstances do not run your inner world.

Start first with your breath. **A deep breath helps create a pause between external stimuli and your response.** Decrease the noise around you. Close your eyes- if you can- even for a moment. Ground yourself- feel your feet on the floor. Slow down your breathing. Imagine your muscles relaxing- especially your neck, your shoulders, your hands, behind your eyes, and your forehead.

This focus on the physical will calm your thoughts and help you center yourself. You can then, choose a deliberate response rather than a reaction.

Choose a mantra- all is well, peace, God is within me, Let go-let God…. whatever works for you. Use it to maintain inner peace- even during turmoil.

"When you change the worrying habit, you are able to enjoy life and deeply experience more peace, passion, energy, and joy." – Dr. Sheri Kaye Hoff, PhD

"The key to success is for you to make a habit throughout your life of doing the things you fear." – Vincent Van Gogh

"Most of us serve our ideals by fits and starts. The person who makes a success of living is the one who sees his goal steadily and aims for it unswervingly. That is dedication." – Cecil B. DeMille

When You Go For Comfortable, You Miss Out on Wonderful

Breakthrough moment: I realized I am wearing a shirt that is the most comfortable shirt I own. The fabric is soft and it is really comfy, but I hate the way it looks on me. I wouldn't wear it out for lunch and if someone stopped over and I was wearing it, I think I would be embarrassed. Other people have told me that they love it on me, but I just don't like it on me at all. A few times I have thought, "Just throw it out".

But the voice inside my head says, "But it is so comfortable, you might not ever have a shirt again that feels this soft and comfy".

Wow, I realized what a great analogy for hanging onto something comfortable even though I don't like it. I am throwing it out today and never putting it on or looking at it again. Message: **Just because something is comfortable doesn't mean it is serving me.**

Lightning bolt: Where else I am doing that in my life? Where are you doing this in your life?

When we keep things around just because they are comfortable, we aren't living into what we really want in our lives, instead we keep hovering around "comfortable, but not good for me".

Some things are comfortable and wonderful. **But often "comfortable" is a way of avoiding expansion and positive change** because our ego minds strive to keep things the same. Our ego minds hate change, it's too scary. Our ego minds want the status quo even if the status quo isn't great.

Our highest level of ourselves wants what is the highest good.

Quiet your ego mind with some soft music, journaling, and meditation. Let your inner guidance speak.

Whether it is a thought pattern, a relationship, furniture, clothing, a struggling business, etc…: **when you go for comfortable, you sometimes miss out on wonderful.**

Command a better story for your best and highest good today. Take action on what is not amazing. Eliminate or tweak what is draining. If it isn't supporting you and making you feel good, it's draining.

Go for it; eliminate all that is merely comfortable.

Freedom! Yeah, baby!

Chapter 4

ACHIEVING GOALS AND LIVING YOUR SUCCESS

Goals and Planning from Now to Next Year and Beyond

You've most likely set goals and you have made quite a few plans. Sometimes everything works out beautifully, other times thinks work out – well – let's just say – not as planned. Both scenarios can be successful. **A change in plans may yield a new goal or new possibility.** In my experience working with clients, planners and goals setters achieve more even if things don't unfold smoothly or there are a few detours.

If the word "goal" sends you running for the hills, or maybe the word gives you that instant feeling of stress, you can still set effective goals and plans in place.

Yes, just setting a goal induces some stress. You might think, "What if I can't do it? What if I fail? Or "I don't even know how to begin". Think of words like "focus" or "objective" or "direction" or "dream" when you think about goals. Don't let anything regarding your past efforts haunt you. Today is a brand new day. **You can think and be whatever you want starting right now.**

Goals and plans can be formally written in great detail or they can be written in a simple bullet list or in whatever way makes the most sense for you. **The key is to find what works for you.**

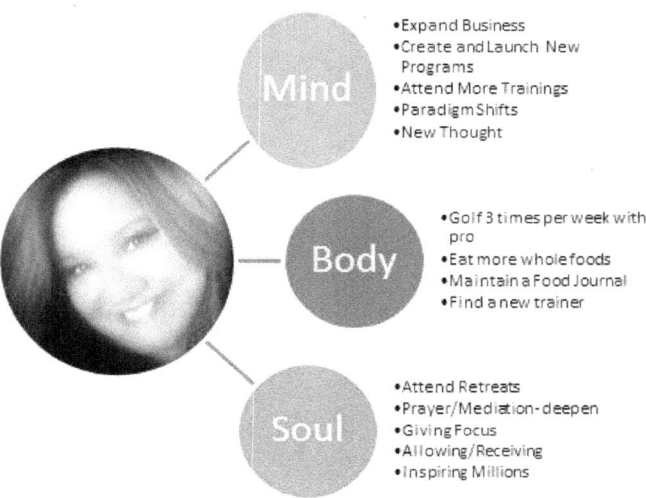

If you know that people who create goals and make plans, achieve more… then, **it makes sense to do it, too**. It is like knowing that brushing your teeth yields a healthier mouth. You do it because not doing it just doesn't make sense.

Key to setting goals so you can **relax into inspired action**:

- Your goals are unique to you and important to you.

- Your goals make your life more exciting.

- Your goals do not create a deep sense of burden or heaviness.

- Your plan is a stretch, but achievable. You concentrate on a shorter list that is significant (not 50 things).

- You create a way to clearly see how to get from point A to point B.

- You hold yourself accountable.

- You reward yourself for milestones.

- You enjoy the process, not just the end result.

- Your goals focus on you living your ideal of your optimized life.

Paint the big picture. What do you want? You get to decide. It is your picture. Reflect on all areas of your life: work, relationships, family, spirituality, intellectual aspects, and your health (add more if you want). Then fill in the details with the daily, monthly, quarterly planned action steps. **Evaluate each action you plan on taking and make sure that it fulfills some part of your plan.** If it doesn't, why is it on your to-do list?

For example, let's look at volunteering at your child's school. If you look at that activity and see it as part of your overall plan to have a strong family bond and a message that education is important, maybe keep that activity. But, if you look at volunteering at your child's school as something you "should" do or maybe you even have a hard time saying "no" when you know it will not work with your schedule, this might be something you take off your list. The beauty of it is that you get to make the decisions about meaning and importance regarding your plans.

Another planning tip: avoid writing things that you have written hundreds of time like" I will lose 20 pounds". Try to come up with a new twist, "I will eat more whole foods." or "I will find movement that I enjoy." (For me, this year, it was discovering a love of golfing. I don't think, "Oh, I am going to exercise" I think "I can't wait to get out on the course.") Another example, "I will pay off all my debts". How about a new twist? "I will open all of my statements in a timely manner." and "I will make timely payments".

Another tip: **Stop worrying about making every moment of your life "productive" and just live it.** If you like watching a few TV shows, go for it. Let yourself have time to just goof around.

Note that in the above graphic, I don't include anything about my family, which is because my family is an area of my life that, for right now, feels really good. I feel great about my relationships. I could include maintain great family relationships in my goals. But it is one area that just feels like it doesn't need to be on a goals chart. (Remember, you get to decide what goes into your goals and planning.)

When you create your plan, keep it front of you. Have it posted on your wall by your desk, keep a copy in your journal, and/or have it in a file that is close at hand. I have a red folder to signify the importance of it.

A Simple Vision Board that Really Works

Here is one of the simplest ways to keep your goals front and forward:

Create a vision board- use very colorful poster board- the background should be what you a drawn to- green, red, and yellow are colors of prosperity… orange- a color for healing… pink- love…. blue – intellectual…purple- spiritual… but you can choose colors that are meaningful to you.

Use a spiritual symbol on your poster. I glued a jeweled cross to mine. And include a meaningful spiritual saying- I used- "God is my Supply". You could use others such as "I am one with the Universe." "The Universe is abundant." The point is that it is meaningful to you.

Put a picture of yourself (a happy one) in the center.

Cut out pics of things that represent what you want to achieve and glue or tape to your poster. Write out or glue positive words on your poster... These go all around your pic… then draw spokes from yourself to each pic and if you like- write a positive affirmation on each spoke.

Put your poster in a place where you will see it often… not where others will see it. Look at it several times during the day.

I know that if I have something on my vision board, it is going to be present in my life, sooner rather than later. There are many different ways to use the vision board idea: Pinterest, a vision photo book, a vision journal, etc.

The Action Plan Process

If you have a goal, you need an action plan. Just creating the action plan starts the momentum rolling in your favor. I have created a list of elements for a good action plan.

Start with a goal. Use a goal that is more narrowed down than- I want to be successful. Success encompasses many goals and each goal will have an action plan. A profit goal might be- Increasing your profits by 10 or 20%.

Information gathering, research, intuition… Next you will start gathering information on this goal. You will be researching on the internet, reading articles, and having conversations with key people. Also, turn inward and listen to your own intuition. It is helpful for you to ask this question before bed. "What is my inner guidance telling me about ways to increase my profits?"

Keep a pen and paper by your made to write down ideas when you wake up. Some information you may have gathered are ideas for marketing, getting new clients, selling products, etc.

Create steps and identify milestones. Based on your information and intuition, create the steps you will be taking to achieve your goal. Choose milestones that will be evidence of progress. So for instance- Your steps might involve ways for creating a new product/service, holding more discovery sessions, getting better at closing the sale, etc. A milestone might be breaking a monthly sales record, adding 5 new platinum clients, etc.

List needed resources. Once you create the steps- you need to know the resources you will need (people, money, time, hard goods, training, etc.). Set a budget regarding the resources. Procure your resources.

Create a timeline. Every goal needs a timeline-this creates a sense of urgency. Even if you end up pushing your timeline out a ways, you are more likely to achieve your goal if you add a date.

Act on steps. Commit to doing something every day- 5 days a week to move towards your goal. Plans mean nothing without action. Stay inspired by remembering why this is your goal in the first place. Be motivated from within.

Celebrate milestones. Celebrating boosts your energy vibration and ensures that you will stay on course.

Evaluation Plan (weekly? 30 days? 90 days? Etc.) Decide what constitutes success... For instance, if your goal is a 20% increase in profits, will you still consider it a success if you achieve a 15% increase. Decide how often you will evaluate your action plan. I suggest evaluating weekly, with major evaluations ant 30, 90, and 180 days at least. More often if you need it. Find an accountability buddy, a mastermind, or a coach who will keep you accountable. In the beginning, you may want to have daily accountability- so your energy remains high.

When you achieve your goal: After implementing your action plan most likely you will have achieved your goal. If you have fallen short, look for the evidence that shows you are going in the right direction.

Decide what's next.... Keep going, build on your momentum.

When Fast is Better than Slow

Do you think it has to take a long time to achieve your goals? What if you could manifest your goals fast- like right away, now, today? **In order to manifest your goals fast, you need first make a**

paradigm shift. Instead of thinking that it takes a long time to achieve goals, what if it were just as likely that you could achieve your goals fast? **Remember time is a man-made concept**.

Often, fast is good. The reason fast is better than slow, is that **momentum is on your side**. Think about the time you decided that today is the day you clean your garage, basement, etc., after waiting for weeks or even months. You get going- and a few hours later, you are done. You wonder why you spent months thinking about doing it or even doing little bits and pieces of the job.

Here is another example. I enjoy writing. **My "relax into inspired action" technique for writing is:** I write when I am inspired, I don't force myself. I easily write several hundred even thousands of words without feeling that it's difficult. One weekend, I decided to challenge myself and see how much I could write over the two day weekend. I wrote over 18000 words. It didn't feel hard. I still went out for dinner, washed clothes, and had time to relax. This was, by far, the most I had written over two days.

And one more example, when I lived in Wisconsin after I was first married, we owned a very large lot along with our house. We had two garages- a brand new garage, and an old, rickety garage. We could not tear down the old garage because it was right on the property line and if we tore it down, we would not be able to rebuild. For two years I stared at that garage. It had several decades' worth of peeling paint.

Finally, I decided I was going to do something about it. I had never painted anything. I researched how to do everything and gathered my supplies. My neighbors laughed at me because I was trying to rescue something so old and dilapidated. My daughter Sonja was 12 months old and refused to stay in her playpen outside. So I scraped paint while holding her in one arm- for one whole day. Then I primed the next day- for the whole day (holding her in one arm). The third day, I painted the whole day (with my daughter in one arm). I set my daughter down once- and she ran through the paint pan and I had little colored footprints on the sidewalk. I did not feel tired. **I was energized even though my arms ached.** The 4th day, I had new garage doors installed with openers. A few weeks later, a relative stopped by and asked when we replaced the old garage and put up a new garage. She was in disbelief when my husband said, "Sheri painted it." I know that if I had stopped at any point, the project would have bogged down and I could have been looking at an incomplete, half done job for another two years.

What are your goals? What could happen fast for you? Challenge yourself today.

What Happens after You Achieve a Major Goal?

Many success articles focus on helping people "get there" – you know, achieve the goal. I, too, have written many articles on how to attain goals. Most of my clients come to me because they have a goal they want to achieve and they want help making it happen. **But what happens after a major goal is achieved?** The logical answer is to celebrate the achievement and then focus on the next goal. And that is also good advice.

However, **there is that in-between time**. After giving an almost herculean effort to achieve an important goal, there is a sense of victory, but also a sense of loss. There is even a sense of emptiness, sometimes. I have experienced this and I see it with my clients, too. When you finish the thing that has occupied so much space in your head and your heart, there is a void. **I sometimes find myself grieving a bit, too when I finish something important.**

I worried about this. I would think- "What is the matter with me?" I even felt guilt. I thought I should be supremely happy and when I would go through sadness after achievement, I frankly, could not understand.

What I have learned is that this is part of the cycle. I see it in myself and my clients. Recognizing that sadness is also a part of the goal achievement cycle helps give a person perspective. I go through it every time I finish a project, finish a book, or any other important goal. **I give myself space and time.** I don't try to talk myself out of it. I honor my feelings and allow my emotions to unfold. I am gentle with myself. I practice excellent self-care. I take baths, listen to soothing music, read books for entertainment, and doodle in my journal.

When you are ready, you can move on to what's
next.

Four Words that Kill Your Success

*Four words that kill your success- "I think I'll
wait."*

**How many times have you received terrific
intuitive guidance and great ideas for the next move
or steps in your life...** you get excited, you do some
research... and then fear pops in and you stop in your
tracks and decide: "well I am comfy right here, right
now" and you put it off again. Ask yourself, if I keep on
doing what I am doing right now, where will I be in six
months? A year? Two years? 5 years?

Yes, I have talked with people who have played
the waiting game with their goals for 5 or more years.
Be courageous... do something today to move you
closer to the life you really want.

If you have been waiting for a long time, it is not too late to start.

All you need is to act on one good choice and you will create an energetic movement in your life that results in many good decisions.

What is that one good choice for you right now? What is your catalyst?

Take a few minutes and write down what you want… then look at it- and write down what you really, really want- it is not always what you think at first.

For example, a person might say, "I want to make more money, but what does that mean? More money could be an extra $50 a month or more money could mean enough money to go beyond struggling, beyond survival mode, and into more than enough; a money place where you can breathe easily and take on the projects that you want to do in life. **See the difference**.

Take a few minutes to get really clear about what you really, really want, then (you probably guessed what I am going to say next) act on it. Take action. Relax into inspired action.

Get Motivated Top Ten List

We all need a little push sometimes to really get motivated in our lives to accomplish our goals and get the most out of each day. Here are ten easy ways to get inspired and motivated right now:

1. Whatever you are doing- find a way to make it fun. Add music, move, change your environment, etc.

2. Open a motivational book to a random page. Read and/or do the exercise.

3. Sleep with motivational books under your pillow. (No, I am not joking).

4. Use inspirational decks of cards. Randomly, throughout the day- shuffle the deck and pick a card – read the inspiration.

5. Visit a homeless shelter or an animal shelter. Interact- help out.

6. Donate (your time, your money, or your things).

7. Do something abundant. Splurge on the best of something- e.g. the best coffee, chocolate covered strawberry, glass of wine, etc.

8. Check out 20 books from the library. (At least one book should be a completely new concept or information for you).

9. When creating passwords- keep them motivational (e.g. happy_2012)

10. Listen to your intuition. Tap your intuition by: Writing down dreams. Spending time journaling. Quietly praying or meditating. Noticing "gut" feelings.

"Don't let anything regarding your past efforts haunt you. Today is a brand new day." – Dr. Sheri Kaye Hoff

"Nothing great was ever achieved without enthusiasm." - Ralph Waldo Emerson

Be in Proactive Mode Instead of Prevention Mode

Be proactive instead of reactive.

Instead of trying to prevent things from happening to you in your business or career (e.g. - a transfer you don't like, a deal falling through), **focus on what it is that you do want.** Write out a paragraph or two starting with the words…. This is what I would like to happen….

When you approach your job or your business (or anything in life) from a place of creativity and choice, you take your personal power back.

My top ten list for being proactive.

1. **Decide** what you do want.

2. Pay attention to your language that you use when describing your work or career. **Use powerful and empowering words.**

3. **Be open** to new ideas and new approaches.

4. Keep the **big picture** in your mind.

5. Learn new skills.

6. Keep your resume/LinkedIn profile up to date.

7. Network with people who are **movers and shakers.**

8. Bring your **A-game** to work or your biz every day. You will feel great.

9. Create a **strategy** for dealing with worry (journaling, meditating, etc…)

10. Get **support** (find a mentor, a coach, a therapist, a friend).

"Instead of trying to prevent things from happening to you, focus on what it is that you do want." – Dr. Sheri Kaye Hoff, PhD

"The most difficult thing is the decision to act, the rest is merely tenacity." – Amelia Earhart

"You can never cross the ocean until you have the courage to lose sight of the shore." – Christopher Columbus

Are you still waiting to get started on your next step?

If you have big goals and you feel like you are not moving forward, ask yourself- "What are the areas in my life where I am hesitating?"

Pause for a moment and write those things down. **Hesitation can become a habit**. When you act on your areas of hesitation, you will often find everything else speeds up and your big goals become a reality.

Sometimes people feel like they are doing research and what is really going on is stalling. Stalling is a result of fear. Fear of change, fear of failure, and/or fear of success. I have even heard fear of fear... We all feel it. Some have more than others, but the true, only way to let fear fall away, is to act.

Play to Your Strengths

Complete this sentence...." Success means to me..."

What came up for you? When you think about success, do you think about the areas in your life that are not working out? If you have great health, do you focus on how you need more money? Or if you have a lot of money, you focus on how you should be fit, etc...

True success involves balance. The traditional approach is to look at your weak areas and try to improve... and that is a good goal. However, take the time to really appreciate what is working. Celebrate the fact that you have something wonderful going on... and that energy will help you in your areas of opportunity. This is a strength based approach to success.

Think of it like this... e.g. If a person can run a marathon which takes training, discipline, and motivation... this person can certainly learn how to manage money more effectively. **Take the success from one area and transfer the skills to another area.**

Exercise: **List your strong areas**. List your areas where you want to improve. Do skills assessment. What skills are evident in your strong, positive areas of your life? How can you use these skills in the areas where you want improvement?

Can and Do People Really Change?

I was watching a rerun of the TV show, Big Bang Theory, and Sheldon made a comment something like… People don't change, they really want to change, but they don't.

My first thought was, "what a depressing way to live life". Then I thought, "Well… quite a few people think that way"

Of course, I believe people can change; it is the basis of my coaching business. I would not be a coach, if I didn't think and know that people can and do change.

**So, why don't more people truly change and
do and be what they want to do and be?**

1. It is easiest to stay the same- for a while, but eventually, the pain will become too great... and change becomes a must.

2. People feel like they keep making the same mistakes over and over and then look for evidence to prove that indeed, it is true, they have not changed. But what happens when you are looking for evidence to your already predetermined conclusion? You prove yourself right.

How about looking for evidence that you have made positive changes? If you are trying to make positive health changes, are you drinking more water? Are you moving a little bit more, even if it is just a few minutes? Did you eat something healthy this week? Etc...

If you are trying to grow your career or your business, have you made new contacts in the last 90 days? Have you had a new idea? Have you learned something new?

You see, **people do change** sometimes because they must and, in the best of times, because they choose to change.

- Instead of counting your setbacks, tally your successes, no matter the size.

- Look at every failed attempt as something learned and part of what makes you so amazing.

- If you can implement small changes... why not consider making big changes, too?

When you make the shift to believing that you can change, you take a huge leap forward. You don't have to be at the top of your class, the smartest guy or gal in the room, or the most beautiful. (If you are all those, chances are that you still have blocks and limiting beliefs that get in the way).

All you need to be and do what you want **is to foster the belief that you can, and then DECIDE to do it**. Decide that you will do it, that you will learn what you need to learn and build the team around you to support you.

"Decision" is genius. When we are on the fence- we are most vulnerable and uncomfortable.

The moment you decide and say- I'm doing it- you unleash unstoppable energy from within.

How to Achieve Long Term Success

You can probably think of someone (maybe even yourself) who demonstrates **long term success**.

What makes him or her special? There are a few key pieces that anyone can implement to ensure long term success.

The first key piece is having a long term success mindset. **See yourself as a person capable of long term success.** Use affirmations, visualization, and positive thinking to embrace the long term success mindset. Get a coach or join a mastermind.

The next element is consistency. **If you want long term success, consistently perform.** This means that if you have a business, you need reach out to clients regularly. If you work in a job, you need to consistently complete projects on time.

Persistence is also vital to long term success. You cannot give up. Make up your mind that you will do and learn what it takes to achieve long term success.

Break out of holding patterns (get unstuck) in order to achieve long term success. **Successful people**

do get stuck, but they stay stuck for shorter periods of time. Take a moment to assess whether or not you are engaging in a holding pattern (avoidance, procrastinating, holding back, not being all in, etc…).

If you have created a bucket list, get it out and see where you stand. If you don't have one, start one. Make changes and/or add to the list. Start on one item. (Learning to golf was still on my list- so I started). When I look at my bucket list, I am steadily checking things off. So, I eventually, I may need to make a new list. I remember when I first created the list, I thought there was no way I would do all of it. I was stretching when I created it. I am so thankful that I stretched myself those few years ago.

How can you stretch yourself and have it still feel good without getting into a desperate energetic vibe?

"Break out of holding patterns (get unstuck) to achieve long term success." – Dr. Sheri Kay Hoff, PhD

When to Be Fierce and Fearless.

Even if you are creating a relaxed vibe in your life and business, there is room for fierceness. I think of a Mama Bear protecting her cubs or a Cat protecting her kittens.

What makes you feel fierce? I feel fierce about standing with my clients as they work on the results they want. My coaching is steeped in happiness, love, purpose, and a deep belief in human potential and a loving God. I'm generally a kind, gentle person, but I do have a fierce side of me- and you do too.

I know that when my clients achieve their goals, they initiate positive change. They make an impact and create ripple effects. When I see people step back from the goals and the results they want and step into fear, that's when my fierceness really kicks in. Why does this make me fiercely and fearlessly stand up for my clients? It's because I know how important their work is. I know what happens when people don't do what they really want to be doing. A few years go by, and they are in almost exactly the same place.

Be fierce about standing up and for your goals, but let go of being attached to the results. Do the work. Work through the fear. And let the results be what they are. The real victory and real change is in the process of fiercely making the impact in the world that makes an important difference to you and those around you. Be fierce about what is important to you. And if you work with clients, be fierce about what is important to them.

You can be fierce without being reactionary. You can be fierce and relaxed. It's about balance.

Please share with me how you relax into inspired action and connect the pieces for a fulfilling life. Visit me on twitter @sherikayehoff or Facebook

Chapter 5

RELAX INTO ATTRACTING CLIENTS

AND

RELAX INTO MORE PROFITS

Relaxing into inspired action also has a ripple effect into client attraction and growing profits for businesses. If you own a business and depend on clients this section will help you relax into attracting clients. If you own a business and depend on product sales vs. signing clients, you will find this section helpful because I address how to relax into growing profits. If you don't own a business or are not thinking about starting a business, you may want to skip to the next section.

When I decided to relax into attracting clients in my own business, I began to love the client attraction process. Before I created this concept in my business, I would get nervous when the business conversation would shift to the terms of a deal. I could feel my throat get tight, and I would start to worry about whether the person in front of me would say "no".

I also extremely disliked the so called "marketing rules". I have a master's degree in business, so it wasn't about knowing how to market, it was more about being in alignment with who I was and how my message was sounding. I didn't like all of that "pain" marketing. I didn't like all the hype. I wanted my marketing to sound like me and to include results that I could deliver. I wanted people to feel like they knew me and trusted me when they read my marketing materials.

I made a decision that **I would only market in a way that felt really good.** If something didn't sound like me, I wasn't going to use it. I also applied this concept to my sales conversations. I had a deep desire to have my free strategy sessions be more than sales conversations. I wanted to deliver real value and respect my prospects and myself during the process. I didn't start giving away free hours and hours of coaching, but I did start using a system that delivered value **and** encouraged people to make a decision to coach with me.

As I became very good at relaxing into attracting clients, I learned that my business clients also wanted to learn this process and my Relax Into Attracting Clients workshops and 2 day virtual retreats were born. These two offerings turned into favorite services. I took the stress and frustration out of the client attraction process and filled the process with a "making a difference vibe". The cornerstone of the process is based in this idea:

There is no good cookie-cutter approach to client attraction.

The process must be customized to what works for each business. There are practical techniques to be learned, but tweaking them and creating customized combinations yields the best results. Your client attraction needs to fit YOU.

Do you need to learn more about marketing? Yes, most likely. Do you need to get over some fear? Probably. Do you need to completely believe in yourself and what you are offering? Absolutely. Often my work lies in **helping clients truly see their own value**. If you don't believe in you, it becomes difficult to have a conversation with someone and have them believe in what you are doing.

If you become relaxed and confident in your client attraction process, you begin to sign more clients. Signing more clients, leads to more revenues, and more revenues should lead to more profits. Handling this piece in your business is critical to your success.

How do you become relaxed about attracting clients? Improving your inner-game is a priority. Getting organized and focused is another priority. The process goes like this:

- Get clear about your own passion, purpose, and goals.

- Understand how you want to make a difference with your business.

- Determine your ultimate result that you deliver. Get this right and on target.

- Create your ideal client profile.

- Create your marketing funnel.

- Define and create your offerings that align with your funnel.

- Create your business plan using your offerings and your funnel.

- Create your marketing plan using your funnel (you can combine this into your

business plan, but many people like to
have this as a separate document).

- Perfect your sales conversation (free
  strategy session, free consultation, etc.).

- Implement your business plan and your
  marketing plan. Be sure to plug in
  milestones in your calendar. Be sure to
  plug in marketing activities in your
  calendar each week. Look twelve to 18
  months out. Without a plan, your efforts
  will be all over the place and less
  effective, or not effective at all.

**If you are in business, you are marketing and
selling.** The key is to find alignment so you are
marketing and selling in a way that becomes **natural
and feels good**.

In each step of the Relax into Attracting Clients
process, you want to use a combination of using your

own intuitive guidance, getting support from an expert,
and doing research. Ultimately, you need to act. The
best plans are nothing without some relaxed inspired
action. Inspired action is beautiful, desperate action is
repelling to people.

If you run a business that doesn't rely on
individual clients, but more on customers who purchase
products, you would substitute perfecting sales
conversations with perfecting product marketing,
delivery, and customer service.

When you use the list above to create and
implement your plan of action, you will see higher
purchase rates and higher sign up rates.

You might be thinking, what should I do with
this list? There might be terms that seem unfamiliar, or
you might be unsure of your efforts in a certain area. I
would love to have a deeper conversation with you. I
invite you to book a complimentary Relax into Making

Money in Your Biz Strategy Session with me. I teach these concepts in my Relax into Attracting Clients Workshop, my Optimize membership program, and my Be the Inspiration Mastermind. I do accept a few one on one clients as well. If you are interested in one on one coaching, contact me right away Sheri@sherikayehoff.com to see when I have an opening coming up.

Chapter 6

CONCLUSION

Relaxing into inspired action and connecting the pieces to live a more fulfilling life are core concepts that I believe are at the heart of conscious business success and success in everyday life as well. Life feels almost like a vacation when you are working daily doing what you love to do, making a difference, and are making money doing it.

The main things that get in your way are truly the things that exist only in your mind. When you master your inner-game and make the effort to learn how to create the life and lifestyle you want, and then take the inspired action steps, I believe you can go as far as you want to go and create what is most meaningful to you.

I have witnessed it. My clients have grown businesses, started businesses, written books, changed fields completely, traveled the world, become happier, made a difference, and truly live inspired lives. All of them have felt fear. All of them have felt self-doubt. All of them felt like giving up at some point. But they kept going, learning, and growing. And ended up doing the things they really wanted to do.

In Happiness,

Sheri

ABOUT THE AUTHOR

Entrepreneurs, solopreneurs, small business owners, coaches, and consultants: **Discover a clear path to creating the business and lifestyle you want**. Relax into increasing your profits doing what you love. Relax Into Attracting Clients. Create more happiness, freedom, and success every day.

Meet Dr. Sheri Kaye Hoff, PhD., MA, B.S, CBC, CPLC, CECS, CSC, CGCL. **The Inspired Action Success Coach.**

Business Coach and Trainer known for **inspiring massive action** and being a catalyst for business growth, attracting clients, and profits in a way that is fun, relaxing, and fulfilling, **Sheri inspires people to the do work they love and make money.** Her clients have a passion for making a difference and making a profit. She is a best-selling author of multiple books including: Keys to Living Joyfully, Be the Inspiration: 7 Ways to Inspire Your World, and Top 11 Ways to Relax Into Making Money in Your Biz. Her books are available internationally and her podcast is global. **Sheri helps conscious business owners to relax into attracting clients and to relax into success.** She uses both spiritual and practical techniques to obliterate blocks and create dramatic change, and she offers customized one on one coaching, group programs, and Optimize- her signature membership program.

She is a business leadership and inner-game expert, and has created coach certification training programs, attracting clients workshops, organizational change management programs for small business, and corporate training and development programs. Sheri has earned a PhD in Holistic Life Coaching and a Master's degree in Organizational Management. She has written extensively on spiritual practices and how they can be applied to business and life as well as law of attraction as applied to business coaching and business growth. She holds a Master's degree in Metaphysics. Sheri has taught business classes at the collegiate level, including organizational change management, human resource management, ethics, and others.

Sheri lost her brother to suicide and experienced setbacks and tragedies that could have stopped her in her tracks, **but she made it her lifetime mission to discover the keys to happiness and success and then share them with the world.** She began her coaching company in 2007 after a very diverse career including everything from being an exercise instructor in her early career, to direct sales, to management, training, and then higher education. She grew up influenced by her mother, an English major, and her father, an

Education Director. Training and development were household values.

She is proof positive that you can combine multiple skills and talents and keep growing and changing. She launched her company because that is the way she felt she could make the biggest difference. She is a supporter and practitioner of the conscious business movement and is a law of attraction business coach. She has coached hundreds of people one on one over the years and thousands have been impacted by her programs. **Her mantra is: Relax into Inspired Action**

Random, little known facts: Sheri was a figure skater as a pre-teen and teen. At one time she thought she wanted to join the Ice Capades. During her first year of college, she wanted to be an archeologist. She has over 30 poems published and a fiction short story.

Married to her best friend for over 20 years, she has three kiddos- and three step kiddos ages 14 to 26 and lives in beautiful Colorado. Sheri loves traveling (remote island beaches are her favorite- among her many adventures, she has encountered a shark while kayaking and snorkeled in a 660 foot deep blue hole). She loves golfing with family, friends, and clients. Reading a book a day has been a life-long habit. Family Sunday dinners are a cherished tradition and regular evenings out with her gal pals are her inner circle support network.

Her mottos: Be Free, Be Happy. Be the Inspiration. Boldly pursue a life of meaning and passion.

www.lifeisjoyful.org

Visit

www.lifeisjoyful.org

For Resources, Solutions,

and

Results

www.lifeisjoyful.org

www.ingramcontent.com/pod-product-compliance
Lightning Source LLC
Chambersburg PA
CBHW070231210526
45168CB00020B/1887